It's Your Turn

Walk In Your Financial Purpose

Tina Smith

ISBN 978-1-64258-178-2 (paperback)
ISBN 978-1-64258-179-9 (digital)

Christian Faith Publishing, Inc.
832 Park Avenue
Meadville, PA 16335
www.christianfaithpublishing.com

Printed in the United States of America

The bible says, "A word fitly spoken is like apples of gold in a setting of silver." If you apply Tina Smith's financial advice, you will find this book to be worth its weight in gold.

-Dr. Derek Grier
Grace Church

Acknowledgements

I'd like to thank everyone who helped this dream become reality and those who encouraged me along the way. Thanks to my parents Ruben and Debra Wright, and sister Tara Wright, for their support no matter where they were in the world. I thank my Grace Church Bishop and Pastor Grier and church leadership for truly teaching the Word of God. A huge thanks to First Command, Dave Surgent, the SEMPER FI District, and the firm's financial advisors who take time with those seeking financial advice, then hire some of us to pay it forward. Thank you to my first editor, Amani Jackson, for helping me see this project though a different lens. I especially want to thank my husband Karshi, and son Anthony, for their sacrifices and unselfishness in sharing me with my clients and now the world.

This book is for everyone who needs reassurance that God's word is still relevant regarding money. Ecclesiastes 7:11 in the Message bible says, "wisdom is better when it's paired with money, especially if you get both while you're still living." Here's where you start to get both ...

Game Plan

I Had to Start Somewhere

I was a twenty-five-year-old Air Force airman when my true financial journey began. I was newly divorced, and I couldn't get a $2 loan without a cosigner. I was very uncomfortable with this position. In time, I was introduced to my first financial advisor. I learned about the importance of getting help in an area I thought I was good in, but I wasn't progressing financially. I figured I could do better so I agreed to learn more. I learned a lot about the military's benefits package. What great benefits the military has to offer young adults! I mean, a 401k plan, health benefits, dental benefits, vision benefits, free food, and free room and board! Listening to my first advisor not only helped me realize what I had but what I was going to lose one day when I left the military. What then?

It's Your Turn!

What benefits package do you have with your current job?

What valuable benefits will you depart with upon leaving your job?

Who can you trust to guide you with planning to replace benefits?

"An intelligent heart acquires knowledge, and the ear of the wise seeks knowledge." (Proverbs 18:15, ESV)

Next Generation

What will you inherit if a parent passes away? Knowledge? Personal belongings? What about financially? Our parents did the best they could with their income. Most of our parents lacked financial knowledge and support on how to leave their children with an inheritance. Today, there are no excuses! Agencies and internet websites are plentiful: pouring out information on not only how to prepare us financially but also our children. I know parents who have a vision of setting up their young children financially for just pennies a day to help pay for college, using mutual funds as assets for secured loans or a down payment for their first home. Those pennies a day could change their children's lives forever. That's just in investments. Consider protecting their future with life insurance too. "Why buy my child life insurance? My child should not die before me!" This is what I hear from some parents. My response? "Of course, no parent expects their children to die before they do. In fact, we want them to live to see their great-grandchildren!" But consider these two things: our children will leave their family one day and there may be illnesses that are hereditary. Medical issues can significantly increase life insurance premiums as people get older. If we can secure their families for pennies a day now and prevent them from having higher life insurance premiums later, why wouldn't we want to do that for them? Putting these things in place are simple and practical ways of leaving a legacy for our children financially.

It's Your Turn!

What type of financial legacy would you like to leave for your child(ren)?

How much can you afford to invest in your child(ren)'s financial future?

What can you commit to today to secure your financial freedom first and then leave an inheritance for your child(ren)?

> *"A good man leaves an inheritance to His children's children, but the wealth of the sinner is laid up for the righteous."*
> *(Proverbs 13:22, NKJV)*

Who Do You Trust?

I often wonder why people who know they need help from a licensed professional never actually meet with one. I realize that finances are a very private matter to many. However, this is the same matter that causes stress, sickness, and can cause divorce in many marriages. One thing I believe is that people can have a hard time with trust in others and even in themselves. They may ask themselves, *"Will I really do what is recommended? Will I actually take an honest look at my finances? Will I give up when I am overwhelmed?"* One thing my bishop teaches us is that the load is lighter when everyone lifts. Caring licensed financial professionals are in partnership with their clients, lifting an equal share. I trusted that my advisors had my best interest in mind, and I trusted myself to be open to wisdom concerning my finances. I'm so glad I trusted my advisors and myself. Who do you trust?

It's Your Turn!

Have you found someone you can trust to provide you with biblical and practical financial advice?
Are you seeing a licensed professional who you can meet with regularly to review your financial plan?
Do you trust yourself to take the practical steps toward securing your financial future?

"Trust in the LORD with all your heart, and lean not on your own understanding; in all your ways acknowledge Him, and He shall direct your paths."
(Proverbs 3:5–6, NKJV)

Are You
Just Looking the Part?

We all have important work to do and we're all busy. Yet are we so busy that we neglect proper money management? Not just in making ends meet but in gaining knowledge about how to manage your money better? Many people decide against help from a licensed professional: they believe their job's earnings will carry them into wealth. This couldn't be further from the truth! If the earnings we do get from our jobs are used correctly and if small sacrifices are established early, then wealth can be obtained. You must allow some income to work for you and your future to achieve your financial goals. Financially intelligent people develop good financial habits and start their financial plans as soon as possible. Keeping those habits can help you enjoy your retirement lifestyle!

It's Your Turn!

What do you believe you are wasting your money on?
What are you willing to sacrifice to start saving money for your financial future?
If you make these small sacrifices, how much money could you save in only two weeks?

"Better to be ordinary and work for a living than act important and starve in the process."
(Proverbs 12:9, MSG)

One Person
Can Make the Difference

Joseph saved the Egyptians from famine. He had keen insight on the Pharaoh's dream and was able to establish a plan to keep them from starving to death during the seven years of famine. How can we also apply this type of keen insight to our financial status? What does God say about our management of finances and debt? Use wisdom to take control of your finances. One person started me on my financial journey. Along the way, I started a family. Other advisors have teamed with my growing family over the years. My family's financial future has been changed forever. This has set the foundation in working in my gift. It all started with one person making a difference for me. How can you make a difference in your family and/or circle of influence?

It's Your Turn!

Could you be the catalyst that would change your family's financial future?

How did your delay in securing your financial future affect you?

Who else does this delay affect?

What's hindering you from taking the next step?

"Let Pharaoh proceed to appoint overseers over the land and take one-fifth of the produce of the land of Egypt during the seven plentiful years. And let them gather all the food of these good years that are coming and store up grain under the authority of Pharaoh for food in the cities, and let them keep it. That food shall be a reserve for the land against the seven years of famine that are to occur in the land of Egypt, so that the land may not perish through the famine."
(Genesis 41:34–36, ESV)

Control Thy Self

Having things in moderation is good. Practicing self-control is hard. If it were easy, everyone could easily do it, right? If we don't exercise self-control and discipline now, our future will be in ruins. My past Starbucks addiction taught me a lesson. A venti Caramel Apple Spice (with extra caramel drizzle in the cup) costs about $4 back when I found myself at Starbucks daily. I'd walk in almost skipping and ready to drink my warm Caramel Apple. Actually, some days, I would be there more than once day to get a drink on the way home from work. I have spent hundreds of dollars a month on drinks (not including food) from Starbucks. If I went to Starbucks once a day for thirty days straight, I would have spent at least $120 in that month. How could I invest that $120 per month for my future? I could have saved $40 for emergencies, invested $40 toward my future and retirement, and lastly, I could have protected my family for $40 per month with a life insurance policy. All I had to do was exercise some self-control in just one area to begin my financial journey. I am so glad I made that choice and took the next step. What about you?

It's Your Turn!

In what areas can you exercise self-control and begin your financial journey today?

What commitment can you make to put toward savings, investments, and/or life insurance to secure your financial future?

> *"Moderation is better than muscle, self-control better than political power."*
> *(Proverbs16:32, MSG)*

I'll Take One
for the Price of Two Please

Wait, what!? Who would be willing to sign up for this offer? I bet no one would! Unfortunately, that's what we do sometimes with our cars when our car loans have high interest rates. An APR over 6 percent for a car loan can be considered high. How does that happen to so many people? Well, car dealers and lenders attract your attention to the low monthly payment instead of helping you understand the bottom line. The bottom line is how much you'll pay for the vehicle after you've paid off your loan. Depending on the interest rate and other conditions of the loan, your $25,000 car could cost you over $40,000! You could have paid for two cars! Bottom line: please look at the bottom line when you are in the market to purchase a car.

If you're in that situation now, there are some things you can do to make the situation better. Consider refinancing the car at a lower interest rate to lower your monthly payment and the bottom line. If you're in the market for a car, only consider what you can afford. You can also get pre-approved for a loan with your local bank or credit union before you go shopping for it. That way, you are in control at all times.

It's Your Turn!

How can refinancing your car lower your monthly payment and the bottom line?
What can you do with your new monthly savings?
What strategies could you implement to save for your next car?

"A prudent person sees trouble coming and ducks;
a simpleton walks in blindly and is clobbered."
(Proverbs 27:12, MSG)

Debt, Debt, and More Debt

Why, oh why, do we continue our toxic love affair with debt? What is it about the debt that attracts us so much? Is it the high-interest rate that we love? Are the annual fees sexy? Or is it simply that we lack one simple principle: discipline. If we can discipline ourselves, can we stop digging our way into more debt? Absolutely! This principle could help individuals where there are no established savings for emergencies and the credit card is reserved for such use. Emergencies will happen, but would you prefer to go into debt to take care of the emergency or use what you already have in savings to handle it? What happens when the lenders say, "You cannot borrow any money due to your debt-to-income ratio"? How will you handle your emergency then? There are some advantages of using a credit card, especially for the rewards programs. However; if you don't exercise discipline, all the reward points in the world won't be able to pay off your debt. Don't misunderstand; I'm not saying that being in some debt is the worst thing ever. What I am saying is that if you use debt as a crutch for instant gratification and in emergencies, that debt is not good for you.

It's Your Turn!

Can you commit to not using credit cards you don't need?

What plan do you have in place to reduce and eliminate your credit card debt?

What advantages can you realize if you free yourself from unnecessary debt?

"The plans of the diligent lead surely to abundance, but everyone who is hasty comes only to poverty."
(Proverbs 21:5, ESV)

White Noise

There are so many opinions on what we should do with our money. We listen to social media, society, broke people, and coworkers about different financial decisions and changes we should consider. How important would it be for a licensed professional to sit face-to-face with you and help determine the financial strategies for you and your family? There is no cookie-cutter path for your financial success since everyone's path is different. It is worth your time and money to sit down with a local licensed professional you trust to help you establish a game plan. We do know that we should seek wise counsel. We seek wise counsel when it comes to our medical condition, our dental condition, car's condition, and home's condition, but we fail to do so with our financial condition. I encourage you to do so in this area as well. When you do, make sure you interview that person because you're hiring them to guide you in financing your future and your dreams.

It's Your Turn!

What bad advice have you received from others?
How will having a trusted professional benefit your financial position?
Who do you trust to help guide you to be financially secure?

> *"Where there is no [wise, intelligent] guidance,*
> *the people fall [and go off course like a ship*
> *without a helm], But in the abundance of*
> *[wise and godly] counselors there is victory."*
> *(Proverbs 11:14, AMP)*

Are You Hungry?

Many people desire to improve their current financial situation. Some want to reduce their debt, others just want to increase their savings, while most want to do what they can in order to retire comfortably and protect their families in the event of a tragic situation. Many people want to improve their current financial situation but won't actually take the necessary steps. Why is that? I have found that eating junk food when I am starving does nothing to truly satisfy my hunger. It's only when I eat healthy food that I am fully satisfied. We listen to others about how to spend our money, whether it be schemes to get rich quick, seeing the latest luxury vehicle commercials, or just living for today. However, the Bible teaches that it's not wise to spend money on things that don't satisfy us: that we should let ourselves eat rich food. Let's eat rich food and listen to the wisest of all concerning how to manage our money.

It's Your Turn!

What are you spending your money on that's not good for you? Why?

How hungry are you to break the bad habits and put that money toward your future?

What does the Bible say about putting money away for the future?

How can you apply that in your life today?

"Why do you spend your money for that which is not bread, and your labor for that which does not satisfy? Listen diligently to me, and eat what is good, and delight yourselves in rich food."
(Isaiah 55:2, ESV)

Surprise! It's Christmas!

This sounds silly, doesn't it? Who doesn't know that Christmas is on December 25 every year? *Spoiler alert!* Christmas is not a surprise! So why do we let it take us by surprise financially? If we wanted to spend $500 on Christmas gifts, would it be easier to spend it all in one paycheck or save small amounts throughout the year? Wouldn't it sound feasible to save $42 a month from January to December and spend the $500 you saved versus taking $500 from that last paycheck before Christmas or getting into debt to buy gifts? Did you ever consider the kings' gifts to Jesus when the true King was born? They were already willing to give what they had and did not borrow from anyone to give their gifts. Let's start the New Year correctly by planning for the surprise of Christmas and save throughout the year.

It's Your Turn!

How much would you like to spend on Christmas gifts?

Have you drafted a budget?

How much will you save per month to spend on Christmas gifts?

What type of stress will the practice of saving alleviate at Christmas time?

How can you apply this to other holidays/birthdays throughout the year?

"When they saw the star, they rejoiced exceedingly with great joy. And going into the house, they saw the child with Mary His mother, and they fell down and worshiped Him. Then, opening their treasures, they offered him gifts, gold and frankincense and myrrh." (Matthew 2:10–11, ESV)

Good Lookin' Out!

I found that I tend to go the extra mile or am more efficient when someone is holding me accountable for my actions. Many people use their spouses, friends, colleagues, parents, support teams, and coaches to keep them accountable for their diet, workout regimen, business plans, and vision boards. However, we don't always seek the same accountability for our financial acts. Since this is an area that has a very important impact on your life, wouldn't it be wise to allow a professional to help sharpen your awareness? I've been sharpened for over seventeen years and now use my gift to sharpen others. There are many licensed financial professionals who are looking out for their clients' best interests to help them achieve their financial goals.

It's Your Turn!

Do you have a coach you trust to help you stay accountable for your financial actions? Why or why not?

How can you help someone else stay accountable?

> *"Iron sharpeneth iron; so a man sharpeneth*
> *the countenance of His friend."*
> *(Proverbs 27:17, KJV)*

To Consolidate
or Not to Consolidate?

When reviewing your budget, find areas of wasted money. Many times, I find that home and car interest rates cause high monthly payments. Having these high payments can stifle financial stability and prevent putting money toward the future. Refinancing these big-ticket items has saved people hundreds of dollars per month. Here's the burning question: "If I refinance, doesn't that obligate me to pay on it longer?" I'm *so* glad you asked! Yes but no! If the conditions are right, you can refinance the current loan amount at a lower interest rate which can lower your monthly payments. There are different strategies that you could use to expedite paying off the new loan with less interest. Additionally, some institutions don't charge you extra for paying the loan off early. We've paid off cars for much less and a lot sooner than expected by refinancing them as our credit improved. Refinancing our home has saved us hundreds of dollars per month as well. We've also been able to use the extra money to purchase quality life insurance, invest more money to enjoy our retirement years, and build our savings for emergencies.

It's Your Turn!

Have you ever considered consolidating your current debt?

What would be benefits of consolidating high-interest debt?

If you chose to consolidate the debt, are there any fees associated with paying the debt off early?

"To everything there is a season, A time for every purpose under heaven: A time to be born, and a time to die; A time to plant, and a time to pluck what is planted; A time to kill, And a time to heal; A time to break down, And a time to build up."
(Ecclesiastes 3:1–3, NKJV)

It All Boils Down to Behavior

In 2004, our financial advisor met with us to help find our wasted money. We considered refinancing our cars at this meeting and discussed why we didn't see the $500 our budget says we should have left over per month. We had no idea where our money was going, but we knew we had nothing to show for all the money we spent. Our advisor challenged us to keep receipts for everything we spent that was outside of our monthly budget and we'd discuss our findings at the next meeting. We couldn't believe what we found. We didn't realize our Starbucks and Arnold Palmer's Half-and-Half addictions were keeping us from achieving our financial goals. We became very cognizant of our spending and still use this strategy today. It's a lifestyle. We have fun and enjoy ourselves but not at the expense of our family's future goals.

It's Your Turn!

What event has shaped your spending habits?
How has paying attention to your spending increased your savings?
What financial goals do you have for you and your family?

> *"A little sleep, a little slumber, a little folding of*
> *the hands to rest, and poverty will come upon you*
> *like a robber, and want like an armed man."*
> *(Proverbs 6:10–11, ESV)*

Why Can't I Do Both?

So you want to decrease your debt. You also want to increase your savings. Why can't you do both? I found the wise answer, thanks to our financial advisors along the way. We looked to pay off my car by making double payments. It sounded like a great idea until our advisor reminded us that we didn't have enough money in savings to handle even the smallest emergencies. We would have to use our credit card to fund the next flat tire, airplane ticket to tend to a family emergency, or anything else. She recommended we save money while reducing debt. So we decided to save based on her recommendation and considered taking some of our savings twice a year to make lump sum payments to reduce our debt. During that time, we were even able to cover an emergency instead of using a credit card to take care of it. We paid our cars off in half the time we thought. Eventually, we were able to enjoy life without car payments-about $800 stayed in our pockets each month. Cha-ching!

It's Your Turn!

What keeps you from saving while paying off debt? What small amount can you commit to saving each month for emergencies while you reduce your debt?

> *"I can do all things [which He has called me to do] through Him who strengthens and empowers me [to fulfill His purpose--I am self-sufficient in Christ's sufficiency; I am ready for anything and equal to anything through Him who infuses me with inner strength and confident peace.]"*
> *(Philippians 4:13, AMP)*

It's Not That Big a Deal

This may be some people's thoughts when it comes to life insurance. There are many different kinds of life insurance, but two are primarily: temporary and permanent. Though many opinions differ on what the best is, the only opinion that should matter is yours. Get educated on what the two types are and what works best for you and your family. Be careful of blanket statements when it comes to your financial situation. Your financial situation is different than your neighbor's so a cookie-cutter solution may not be suitable for your household. There are some basic differences between the two types that should be used as a foundation of knowledge. Talk with a licensed professional about the details, but here are a few tips:

- Temporary insurance is normally offered through your employer and a portion of your premium (if not all) can be paid through your employer. Some organizations allow you the "take it with you" option once you leave your job, but you can expect to pay higher monthly premiums after you've left.

- Temporary insurance can be offered in many variations. As you continue to keep temporary insurance, you can expect to pay more in monthly premiums as time goes on.
- Permanent insurance is normally offered outside your employer and is based on your own personal health conditions. The purpose is for the insurance to expire with you, not before you.
- Permanent insurance can offer options that temporary insurance do not: like cash value and other options you can use as long as you own the policy/policies.

Each type can be effective if used in the correct circumstances, but it would be beneficial to speak with a licensed professional face-to-face to hear about the details that fit you and your finances. Share what is important to you and find out what type matches your conditions best. Either way, life insurance is a great way to protect your family and leave a legacy.

It's Your Turn!

Do you think you need life insurance? Why or why not? How would owning life insurance benefit your family? Who can speak with you to find out what type(s) benefit you most?

When will you be able to obtain life insurance to protect your family?

> *"Now the wife of one of the sons of the prophets*
> *cried to Elisha, 'Your servant my husband*
> *is dead, and you know that your servant*
> *feared the Lord, but the creditor has come to*
> *take my two children to be His slaves.'"*
> *(2 Kings 4:1, ESV)*

Notes

So Why Get Life Insurance Anyway?

M ost people agree that life insurance is a necessity. Most don't know why exactly, or what types are available, and how it can work for you if disaster strikes. Here are some reasons why we have life insurance:

- Replace income: If you were to pass away, what income would you be accruing? Unless you have other options already in place, your income stops upon your passing. Life insurance gives your family a lump sum to do what's needed for them to carry on without stressing out about how they'll make it without your income.

- Leave a legacy: What financial legacy are you leaving your family? Are you leaving them with money to fund college, future homes, and other things that will set your family in a positive financial position?

- Eliminate debt and keep a roof over the family's head: If you passed away, how would your family pay for a place to live and pay off remaining debt? Will they be able to afford the monthly obligations on one less income?

- Other options: Some insurance types allow you to borrow cash against your insurance or keep some coverage while not paying the monthly premium. You may use these options later. I appreciate having options regardless of the situation.

These are reasons we wanted to protect our family through life insurance if anything ever happened. Why are you protecting your family?

It's Your Turn!

How much life insurance do you have?
Is this coverage enough?
How much insurance do you need?
How much will you commit to in monthly premiums to take care of your family?

"Poverty and disgrace come to him who ignores instruction, but whoever heeds reproof is honored."
(Proverbs 13:18, ESV)

Notes

Get It While You Are Young

Have you ever seen the commercials where the family comes home from the funeral of a neighbor or close friend? In these commercials, they discuss how the person who passed away didn't have life insurance and that they should consider getting insurance now but wondered if they can afford it based on their age and health conditions. This is a tough conversation to have, especially if that person is on a fixed income. However; this conversation could have been a lot easier if it happened when that person was young. Most people don't realize how inexpensive life insurance can really be if they get it while they're young and healthy. Many young people may prefer spending money on looking good and driving nice cars rather than using a small amount for a life insurance premium to save money in the long run. I was so healthy twenty years ago. I had no medical ailments and a very thin medical record. I can't say that today! I'm thankful I spoke with a licensed professional while I was young and learned about the benefits of getting life insurance while it was inexpensive. Those medical questions on the insurance application were very easy to answer back then, but today, I'd have a lot more explaining to do and would have to pay more.

It's Your Turn!

What's causing you to pause about getting life insurance?

Who can you speak with face-to-face about getting the coverage you need?

How has your health changed over the past ten years?

Why do you think you need life insurance today?

"One pretends to be rich, yet has nothing; another pretends to be poor, yet has great wealth."
(Proverbs 13:7, ESV)

We're Out of Toilet Paper!

These are five words no one wants to hear, especially while needing toilet paper at that very moment. I have yet to hear these words because my fear of them keeps me purchasing toilet paper, forgetting about the extra rolls I've placed in every bathroom, the extra pack in the linen closet, and the extra-value-sized pack in the garage. That's a lot of toilet paper! However, when will there be a time we won't use it? We'll eventually use it, especially in our house. For some reason, I feel better knowing I have more than enough toilet paper in the house like we're safe from catastrophe. I find I will buy extra while I'm shopping for groceries using proper planning versus heading to the 7-11 and paying five times more when disaster struck. So why do we wait to get life insurance? Not everyone values this most crucial part of a financial plan. When a client dies, I help the surviving spouse put the pieces back together. There are these five words I never want to hear from a surviving spouse: we didn't have life insurance.

It's Your Turn!

What keeps you from obtaining life insurance outside your employer-sponsored coverage?

What plan do you have to compliment and/or replace your employer-sponsored coverage?

How will your family sustain without your income if you pass away?

> *"The crown of the wise is their wealth,*
> *but the folly of fools brings folly."*
> *(Proverbs 14:24, ESV)*

Get It While You Are Young (The Remix)

I regularly encourage young people to start a 401k plan with their employer as soon as they're eligible. This is extremely beneficial because it allows you to put away money before you get your check and are tempted to do something else with that money! If someone decides to participate in their 401k plan for twenty-plus years, they may be able to secure themselves in a better position to enjoy their retirement. If they start contributing early before marriage, kids, mortgage, and all the other things life comes with, then they will probably continue to invest. I'm glad I started before my life became more complex. I became more disciplined to live without the extra money and continue to live beneath my means, which allowed more contributions when I got promotions or pay raises. The trend continued as a husband, kid, homes, and everything else came along.

Most people I have spoken with aren't sure about what is in their 401k, what funds are available, or how to maximize it. It's worth your time to speak with a licensed professional face-to-face so that they may show you details about your plan that you may not know. Until then, here a few things you'll want to find out:

- Is there an option for a Roth 401k? Most companies don't offer a Roth 401k plan, but a few do (i.e., federal government). This option allows you to invest without paying taxes when you take the money out of the 401k after 59½ years of age. This is unlike traditional 401k, where you pay taxes on the end result.
- What list of funds can you invest in? Some companies start employees in a default fund, which could be very conservative. This means what you put in is not much more than what you get out many years later. After a few years, you may not be impressed with the growth and may find it useless. However, talking with a licensed professional would help you determine a strategy that would help you best.
- Does your employer offer a match? Some companies will match your contributions up to a certain percentage. For instance, if

you invest 5 percent of your gross income, your company may invest 5 percent of your gross income as well into your 401k plan. However, if you contribute only 1 percent, you have capped your employer's matching contribution to 1 percent. Let's put this in dollars. If you contribute $500 in one year and your company gives a matching $500, you and your employer have invested $1,000 in your 401k. Yet if you give $100 that year, you've obligated your company to match $100. You and your employer have contributed $200 that year.

- Also, find out where your company will match. Will they match your Roth or traditional 401k or a safe harbor cash account? The key is to start even if you start off small. You can build your empire as you go.

It's Your Turn!

Are you participating in your 401k plan? Why or why not?

If so, do you know if you're being conservative, moderate, or aggressive in your plan?

What changes can you make to your 401k plan now to help you enjoy retirement without financial worries?

"Does anyone dare despise this day of small beginnings? They'll change their tune when they see Zerubbabel setting the last stone in place!" Going back to the vision, the Messenger-Angel said, 'The seven lamps are the eyes of GOD probing the dark corners of the world like searchlights.'"
(Zechariah 4:10, MSG)

It's Even Better
When You Work Together!

A couple consists of two people. These two people should share one vision financially. However, some couples on the opposite sides of the financial spectrum. One person wants to save while the other wants to spend. One person wants to sacrifice for the future while the other would prefer to be instantly gratified. I've found that the most successful couples do better financially when they have established goals and plans together. While my husband and I were dating, we talked about money, credit, credit scores, and financial goals. You read that right: while we were dating. We shared many of the same financial values and could see the other's point of view even when we didn't agree on how to reach those goals. This group of discussions was a determining factor in our decision to take our relationship to the next level. As we grew our financial portfolio, we knew we couldn't go in opposite directions. As we work together and with our advisors over the years, we've become proud of what we have accomplished, but we expect to build more toward our retirement and beyond. If we didn't seek God's Word, get professional advice, and join together in this journey, we would not be well on our way to reaching our goals together!

It's Your Turn!

When was the last time you spoke with your spouse about finances?

What goals have you set?

What plan do you have in place to support your goals?

How has God's Word and professional counsel catapulted you to the next level of achieving your financial goals?

"Again, if two lie together, they keep warm, but how can one keep warm alone? And though a man might prevail against one who is alone, two will withstand him—a threefold cord is not quickly broken."
(Ecclesiastes 4:11–12, ESV)

How Did We End Up Here?

Moses was the leader of the Israelites. He led the people as God directed but spent forty years in the wilderness. I can imagine the Israelites saying things under their breath and rolling their eyes as Moses directed them. I can hear some of them say, "Weren't we here 20 years ago? How'd we end up here—again?" Well, sometimes we can ask those same questions about our financial situation. Just when we get on track, we get knocked off again. *Spoiler alert!* The enemy doesn't want us to live life more abundantly as the Word of God promises. He wants us to be discouraged, stay broke, and poor, which is not living the life of a King's kid. But the devil is a liar! We must push through and continue to manage our money responsibly so that we can have the life we really want and bless others along the way. I've been discouraged in the aftermath of a setback, but I've had to quickly regain positive ground and go forward. Everything, as it always does, turned out all right. You lose if you quit. Never quit!

It's Your Turn!

When was the last time you had a financial setback? How did you handle it?

How committed have you become over the years to continue reaching your financial goals and building wealth?

How have you encouraged someone this week to continue managing money the right way?

"The thief does not come except to steal, and to kill, and to destroy. I have come that they may have life, and that they may have it more abundantly."
(John 10:10, NKJV)

You Can't Change
What You Avoid

Oh, I learned this the hard way. Sometimes, being passive gets you nowhere. In my profession, a couple of bad seasons can get anyone to question if this is what they're supposed to be doing. I know I've had to ask God a couple times because I thought I misheard His voice after a few bad moments. The longer I ignored the signs and dismal circumstances, the longer I stayed in these conditions and nothing changed. It's not until I stare the circumstances in the face, wrap my mind around them, write down a plan, and get active that things turn around for me. This concept could also be applied to how you may see your debt. If you ignore the balances and just stomach the minimum payments, you'll continue to live in fear. When you're tired of being scared to face it, you'll be able to attack it and become debt free.

It's Your Turn!

How long has it been since you last mustered up the courage to face your debt?

How do you feel about having to pay what you owe? What written plan do you have that you can commit to in order to eliminate your debt?

"He who has a slack hand becomes poor, but the hand of the diligent makes rich." (Proverbs 10:4, NKJV)

Emergency Savings: The Linchpin

Linchpin is defined as something that holds the various elements of a complicated structure together. Finances and managing them can be complicated, right? What's the primary thing that holds a financial plan together while reducing your debt? What is the one thing that could be ignored most in a reduction plan? Most people focus so much on getting out of debt that they don't remember what got them there in the first place. In some cases, it was the unexpected emergency flight back to family, a car repair, a home repair, or sudden medical expenses. Once that charge to the credit card happened, why not add one more to the list of upcoming charges? Is it possible that if we had been proactive and saved for emergencies our debt situation may have been different? Now that we are in debt, let's look to get from under the bondage by saving. What? Yes! Think about it. If all of your extra money is focused toward paying off debt, what will you lean on in the case of emergency? *Spoiler alert!* The same debt you're trying to get free from. It's worth putting up small amounts of savings for emergencies before they happen versus being unprepared. Start working with what you have.

It's Your Turn!

What has been your solution for recent emergencies? How has that worked for you?

What are you willing to sacrifice to make sure you have adequate savings in case of emergencies?

How can having emergency savings help you achieve your financial goals?

"And Elisha said to her, 'What shall I do for you? Tell me; what have you in the house?' And she said, 'Your servant has nothing in the house except a jar of oil.'"
(2 Kings 4:2, ESV)

Payday Loans:
The Slave Master

Well, this one is near and dear to my heart. Why? My heart breaks every time I talk with someone who is seeking ways to get out of debt and have payday loans as part of their debt. I literally want to cry. I recognize that some of us are in a bind and really need this. However, this should not be your pinch hitter in emergency situations. Consider this: if you borrow $300 from a payday loan agency, you are obligated to repay the loan in twelve low monthly payments. Did you realize the schedule causes you to repay your $300 by paying them over $1,000 after twelve months? Your interest rate on this particular loan could be up to 700 percent. Does that sound like a good deal to you? Here's a better idea: save $50 a month, and you'll have $300 in six months. You would have this $300 you needed in the same emergency, and guess what? You don't owe anyone!

It's Your Turn!

If you have a payday loan, what plan do you have in place to pay it off as soon as possible?
If you had a savings, would you have gotten a payday loan?
What can you do to prevent from depending on payday loans again?

> *"The rich rules over the poor, and the borrower is the slave of the lender."*
> *(Proverbs 22:7, ESV)*

Rent-to-Own Contracts: The Slave Overseer

We see the commercials about the opportunity to rent-to-own furniture, appliances, name-brand purses, rims, and other things. The low payments are attractive, but the overall payment can be quite daunting. I've done a quick analysis of the rent-to-own system for a sixty-five-inch television. Now a sixty-five -inch television is a need, right? This TV could be bought outright for $1,800 or you could rent-to-own it for only $130 per month for twenty-four months. That low payment sounds real good! But when I did the math for the twenty-four-month plan, I found that I would actually be paying over $3,100 for the same TV I could have bought for only $1,800. As we consider these options, we cannot look at the monthly payments alone. Those will almost always look very affordable and attractive. Look at the bottom line and find how much you'd actually pay in total. Charging you extra is a profit for them while keeping you in bondage.

It's Your Turn!

If you are in a rent-to-own contract, how can you repay this off as soon as possible?

How can you keep from obtaining things in a rent-to-own fashion?

How will considering the bottom line change your decisions going forward?

"If a man vows a vow to the Lord, or swears an oath to bind himself by a pledge, he shall not break His word. He shall do according to all that proceeds out of His mouth." (Numbers 30:2, ESV)

Work until You Die

This doesn't sound appealing me at all! I don't know about you, but I envision myself and my husband traveling together to see family, distant friends, and visiting other countries in our retirement years. I see us riding in our first luxury car as we've dreamed, only on the nice summer weekends. Like me, I'm sure you've realized your normal income won't elevate you to wealth. Thankfully, there are many avenues that, if used correctly and over time, will help you create the wealth you desire in your later years. My family chooses to sacrifice small amounts of our income in the present in order to allow it to build over time for our future. Your employer's 401k, pension plan, other investments, and various types of life insurances will help you build the wealth for retirement and beyond. Some of us don't expect to work ourselves to death because some of us choose to use these vehicles properly. Let's live!

It's Your Turn!

Do you plan to work until you drop dead? If not, what goals do you have for retirement?

What's stopping you from using small amounts of your income toward your future?

What plan do you have to replace your employer's benefits when you leave your current place of employment?

"He also who had received the one talent came forward, saying, 'Master, I knew you to be a hard man, reaping where you did not sow, and gathering where you scattered no seed, so I was afraid, and I went and hid your talent in the ground.'"
(Matthew 25:24–25, ESV)

I'll Take Social Security at Age Sixty-Two

I f so, why? Do you have no other source of income for retirement? If not, applying for social security as soon as you are eligible may be the best decision for you, but you can change that if you act now while you are young. If you plan for your future, you'll be able to take this government benefit at the age of your choice versus taking the benefit just to survive. Use the available investment vehicles to grow wealth now so that you won't be forced to take it at your age of eligibility: when you'll get the least amount monthly. Each person has a retired age as recognized by the government. My age is sixty-seven. I can get my full retirement pension at this age. However, my benefit increases 8 percent per year if I wait until age seventy. That's an extra 24 percent! Why wouldn't you want to wait? People are living longer, so some may like the higher pension the last fifteen to twenty years of life. If your financial behavior is good during the working years and has helped you grow wealth, then waiting three extra years to receive the maximum benefit shouldn't hurt your family financially. In fact, it will guarantee that you get the most money in later years. Who doesn't want that?

It's Your Turn!

What vehicles do you use to grow your wealth?
How can you increase your wealth using your current income?
Have you increased your contributions to these vehicles as you get a pay raise or eliminate debt?

> *"By your wisdom and your understanding*
> *you have made wealth for yourself, and have*
> *gathered gold and silver into your treasuries;"*
> *(Ezekiel 28:4, ESV)*

Freeze!

The headlines read, "New administration freezes federal government hiring." This is a huge deal in the DC/Maryland/Virginia (DMV) area. Many federal employees are located in the DMV and other metropolitan cities across the United States. People from all walks of life, including our veterans, are directly affected by this. I do believe this is a lesson for those who believe it will never happen to them. I'd like to quote my husband here: "Work for the best. Prepare for the worst." The word *prepare* sticks out to me, as it should for you, when speaking about your finances. Let's go back and learn from the ant that used wisdom to prepare for the winter. *Spoiler alert!* Winter always comes. Are you prepared for the freeze?

It's Your Turn!

What can you do while things are going well to prepare for tough times?

Who can you trust to show you biblical and practical principles to be prepared financially?

How can being prepared for winter help you during these times?

"Go to the ant, O sluggard; consider her ways, and be wise. Without having any chief, officer, or ruler, she prepares her bread in summer and gathers her food in harvest." (Proverbs 6:6, ESV)

I'll Cross That Bridge
When I Get to It

When it comes to truly preparing for your financial future, planning is indeed key. There are so many opportunities we can take advantage of now that can help us prepare correctly. Not everyone has the courage to prepare though. Some people have the courage to plan but not enough courage to take steps in implementing a financial plan. This fear of taking practical, small, but crucial steps can make the difference between enjoying retirement and working longer than desired. Many work into their retirement years because they cannot afford to stop working. They decided to cross that bridge when they got there. When will they actually cross over to retirement? Possibly never. I have a better idea. Build your own bridge by planning your financial future and cross that bridge on your terms!

It's Your Turn!

What fear is holding you back from planning for your financial future?

What dreams do you have that require a monetary source of some kind?

Why haven't you begun planning for your financial future already?

*"Wealth gained by dishonesty will be diminished,
but he who gathers by labor will increase."
(Proverbs13:11, NKJV)*

Show Your Work

I love math! If I help my son with his math problems at home, I enjoy seeing him work out the problems. Sometimes, he decides not to use his scratch paper to work toward the right answers. He tries to find shortcuts, which doesn't work out well. When actually utilizing his scratch paper to show his work, we can see what went right and what didn't. He arrives at the correct answer when he takes advantage of available resources. Same goes for our finances. Having a written financial plan shows the work ahead and allows you to take steps toward your goal. The Bible does give advice about writing a vision. It also encourages us that when we write it we tend to take it more seriously, and it's more likely to be followed. Write your vision and put the Word on it. Are you ready to show your work?

It's Your Turn!

What keeps you from writing down your financial plan or vision?

Do you have faith in God, and in yourself, to follow the plan?

If you have a written plan, when was the last time you reviewed it?

> *"And the Lord answered me: 'Write the vision; make it plain on tablets, so he may run who reads it. For still the vision awaits its appointed time; it hastens to the end—it will not lie. If it seems slow, wait for it; it will surely come; it will not delay.'"*
> *(Habakkuk 2:2–3, ESV)*

Start from Zero

If zero is where you are, start there. The Bible encourages us not to despise small beginnings. You have dreams and goals. I'm cheering for you to reach them! However, you don't reach them without starting from the beginning, at zero. Many are attracted to the opportunity of owning investment properties. What an opportunity, if you have money and assets available to use them in an investment property venture. In my state of residence, Virginia, an investment property could cost more than $30,000 as a down payment. This means that you must come with the lump sum of money when you purchase the property. Not to mention, you may have to provide more at closing, which could be only eight weeks from purchase. Your credit is investigated like never before! Can your credit withstand this process? This is why it's imperative to start at the foundation of your financial plan. Decrease debt, increase savings. These two steps alone will help improve your credit. I want you to thrive and experience the abundant life that God purposes for us. Otherwise, I would've kept this book to myself. But you have to start at zero.

It's Your Turn!

What steps are necessary to achieve your financial goals and dreams?

What keeps you from taking the first or next step?

What are you willing to give up to achieve your dreams?

"The hands of Zerubbabel Have laid the foundation of this temple; His hands shall also finish it. Then you will know that the LORD of hosts has sent Me to you." (Zechariah 4:9, NKJV)

Don't Let It Stop You

Paralysis. This is a strong word that is defined as a state of helplessness, stoppage, and activity, or inability to act. Does this describe your financial health? Even if this is true, you cannot continue your financial journey in this state. You will never reach your goals if you are financially paralyzed. Should you approach a speed bump, hurdle, or mountain, you cannot allow paralysis to stop you! Keep moving, keep pushing, and focusing on your goal of reducing debt, increasing savings, and implementing other key components in a comprehensive, solid, and sound financial plan. Remember, when you give up, you lose.

It's Your Turn!

What situation in your life caused you to be paralyzed concerning your finances?

What commitment can you make today to move on from your paralysis?

What goals do you have that will motivate you to get moving and act toward reaching your financial goals?

> *"For I know the plans I have for you, declares*
> *the Lord, plans for welfare and not for*
> *evil, to give you a future and a hope."*
> *(Jeremiah29:11, ESV)*

Gift

Who's Hating Who?

Who are you allowing to hold you back from God's purpose in your life? What is it that God has purposed for you to do? Are you your own hater? I've found my life to be more abundant in all areas only when I began to work in my purpose. Nothing held me back. Lack of money or income would have, but my husband and I implemented a plan to prepare us for that next chapter in my life. The strategy we implemented kept us afloat financially while transitioning from a steady to a fluid income. We sacrificed wants until my income stabilized. If lack of money is why you're not confident walking in your purpose, develop a strategy to use your income from your job to fund your dream! You can accomplish your goal with strict focus and discipline.

It's Your Turn!

What's your purpose?

Why haven't you begun walking in your purpose yet?

What relationships are hindering you from walking in your purpose?

How much money can you commit to begin saving today to help finance your purpose?

If you only get the foundation laid and then run out of money, you're going to look pretty foolish. Everyone passing by will poke fun at you: 'He started something he couldn't finish.'"
(Luke 14:29–30, MSG)

Helping Hand

In 2000, someone helped me recognize that I could be doing better financially. I was taking a college course with a first sergeant on my base in North Dakota. After class one night, he asked the then twenty-five-year-old Tina what I was doing with my money. This is the one question that set my life on a new path. From there, my first financial advisor set me on the right path. I will never forget those two men who pointed me in the right direction financially. If I did not meet them and they did not inspire me to act, my family's financial situation today would be in dire straits. Shoot, all I knew was how to be cheap and save a few dollars per check. I would not know any of the opportunities available to me if it had not been for them. The years that followed trained me on how I would eventually use my gift. Had I not been faithful to my journey, I would not have been recommended to become a financial advisor. Now, I help and inspire family, friends, old colleagues, strangers, and even you to take the steps necessary to grow your future financially.

It's Your Turn!

Who do you inspire to improve their current financial situation?
Who are you going to inspire next?
Who/what inspired you to read this book?
Why is inspiring others important to you?

> *"Two are better than one, because they have a good reward for their toil. For if they fall, one will lift up His fellow. But woe to him who is alone when he falls and has not another to lift him up!"*
> *(Ecclesiastics 4:9–10, ESV)*

Who Will You Believe?

Opinions: everyone has some about something. I like facts and place them higher than an opinion any day. In the Bible, the Pharisees had their opinions about Jesus and how he operated. Jesus operated in His authority and spoke the Words of God. His statements were factual. So when the Holy Spirit shared with you about your gift and how to use it, did you hear a negative opinion from yourself? When you talk to someone else, were they pessimistic? Who will you believe? Jesus was completely confident in Himself to operate in His authority. We should be confident too. Invest in yourself, your gift, and trust God to see you through. These steps will help you realize the dreams and desires He placed in you.

It's Your Turn!

How confident are you that the Lord has spoken to you about your gift?

What small changes can you make to improve your gift?

What are your short- and long-term goals for using your gift?

> *"Being confident of this very thing, that*
> *He who has begun a good work in you will*
> *complete it until the day of Jesus Christ."*
> *(Philippians 1:6, NKJV)*

Why I'm So Serious

As I think about my family, I think about my motivation for a more abundant life. I am motivated to be all I can be according to God's purpose so that God gets the glory first, but then, that my family won't ever be limited by something as small as money. I'm also motivated as I consider our communities and the economy. So many people want more in and out of life but can't seem to put their finger on why they aren't experiencing that. I find that information isn't looking for anyone, it's just waiting to be found. Most people don't know about financial keys to a common person's success unless they have a chance to speak with someone about their financial situation. I spend some nights and weekends away from my two favorite boys to be the conduit between the information gap. I always say that I'm saving the world one client at a time. I can't save it doing nothing. And neither can you.

It's Your Turn!

What has God called you to be?
What/who motivates you?
What can you commit to today to move closer to what God's purpose is in your life?

"Salt is good and useful; but if salt has lost its saltiness (purpose), how will you make it salty? Have salt within yourselves continually, and be at peace with one another." (Mark 9:50, AMP)

Why Keep It to Yourself?

You know. You know what the Lord has shown you: about your purpose, the business He told you to open, yet you are afraid. You ignored God's unction because of fear. The Bible teaches that fear is not from God. Paul encourages Timothy to be courageous. So I will be your Paul. Be courageous! When was the last time the Lord spoke to you and you obeyed but failed? It never happened! Don't keep your gift to yourself. Someone needs the fruits of the gift that you have. Use wisdom and move toward what God has shown you. You might not be able to quit your job right now and support yourself financially, but put aside a portion of your job's pay to start your business today. If you look to start it in seven to ten years, you may want to consider investing the money in a mutual fund which allows that money to grow until you are ready to launch. The Bible warns us to count the cost, so heed the Word of God and do so. Be focused until you open your business, walk in your purpose, and watch God do what He does best—honor His promises. However, you have to take the steps toward His promises. Go!

It's Your Turn!

What keeps you silent about your gift and purpose?
When do you want to open your business using your
gift and purpose?
How can you commit to being courageous today?

> *"For this reason I remind you to fan into flame*
> *the gift of God, which is in you through the laying*
> *on of my hands, for God gave us a spirit not of*
> *fear but of power and love and self-control."*
> *(2 Timothy 1:6–7, ESV)*

Have You Lost
Your Mind?

N o, actually I found it. I remember my last twen-
ty-five months in the military very vividly. The
Lord kept speaking to me about leaving the military
in arguably the worst economy in recent memory. I
wasn't getting promoted, things were changing, and
the force was shrinking. I wasn't having fun anymore.
I felt peace about leaving as time went on. We could
afford to be a single-income family, so I was free to
leave financially. I was recruited by companies, then
doors were slammed in my face. I finally listened to
what I had been sensing: to find my purpose and work
in it. But what was it? During some conversations, I
started thinking about the people I helped over the
years in the area of finance. I've helped people in my
circle of influence with their budget, how to shop
for groceries, and ball out on a budget. I also knew
how to get out of debt since we've done that twice.
I wanted to impact the world in a special way, but I
couldn't see myself doing it from the cubicle. Then
I sent one e-mail, and it changed my life. That door

was blown to smithereens. I wasn't the best qualified since I don't have any finance degrees, but I had more passion about this subject than anyone else I came in contact with. In all, being a financial planner has been the absolute most rewarding and compensating profession I've ever engaged. If I hadn't lost my mind to leave a steady income to work in my purpose, what would you be reading right now?

It's Your Turn!

How many times have you thought about leaving your profession for your passion?
What has God given you to be passionate about?
What steps can you commit to in order to spend more time, if not all your time, in your passion?

> *"She came and told the man of God, and he said, 'Go, sell the oil and pay your debts, and you and your sons can live on the rest.'"*
> *(2 Kings 4:7, ESV)*

You Belong

In a trip to the United Arab Emirates, I saw so many beautiful buildings, people, and vehicles. We dined at some of the world's finest restaurants and saw seven-star hotels! As we walked into Burj Khalifa, Burj Al Arab, and many other places, we were greeted as if we were also some of the most important people in the world. Being in settings like these, we may begin to question if we belong. There was no question from those who greeted us if we truly belonged. However, I found that the only person who questioned my credentials about belonging there was me. The Bible says that our gifts will make room for us and put us before great men. If we indeed exercise our gifts, we will conduct ourselves and prepare ourselves for situations to come. My father likes to say, "Act like you've been in the end zone before." So as you hone in on your purpose and begin protecting your gifts, practice acting like you scored a touchdown already.

It's Your Turn!

What gift are you keeping that could change the world?

In that gift, are you walking in your victory?

What keeps you from believing God's Word about your gift making room for you and putting you before great men?

> *"A man's gift makes room for him, and brings him before great men."*
> *(Proverbs 18:16, NKJV)*

Look, but Don't Touch

During an overseas trip to one of the wealthiest countries in the world, United Arab Emirates, my husband and I visited eight malls. In every mall, we saw Tiffany's & Company, Cartier, Hermes, Rolex, Audemars, and the list goes on! We saw so many diamond necklaces, earrings, rings, watches, and bracelets that we had to wear sunglasses after a while! We were in awe of all the luxurious jewelry we were seeing! It was all so beautiful that it's easy to see how people leave there broke! The Bible says we must count up the cost before you start a project so you may finish it and not become a laughing stock. We must do the same in our businesses. We must remain focused on the gifts God has given us to use to help others. Now we could have easily disregarded all the goals we set for our financial futures and our purpose in God to be super fancy and adopt the You Only Live Once principle during our trip. Instead (and thankfully), we set a budget to have our fun, and boy, did we! Even then, we must balance ourselves to finish what we've been assigned and not let our nonchalant attitude be the reason we gave up on

God, our gift, and His purpose for our lives. Get and stay focused.

It's Your Turn!

What lack of discipline is keeping you from starting your business and follow your gift and purpose?
What are you willing to sacrifice to accomplish His good and perfect will for your life?
What are you willing to commit to today to take a step toward fulfilling your purpose?

> *"For which of you, intending to build a tower, does not sit down first and count the cost, whether he has enough to finish it."*
> *(Luke 14:28, NKJV)*

And These Things Will Be Added

This Bible passage is one that, quite frankly, I've been ignoring. My focus has really been on seeking God's kingdom and it should be first. Yet let's remember that as we seek God's kingdom things and stuff will come to us. What things and stuff exactly? That's something that I had not considered at all until my husband and I began to talk about this verse. This is a verse that he had studied before and he received a revelation of its totality. What he shared with me was pretty eye-opening yet still hard for me to wrap my mind around. So I'm stuck on seeking the kingdom and forgetting the rewards that come from seeking His kingdom. We should remember that there are rewards not just in heaven but on earth! However, the rewards should not be the focus. We should be seeking the kingdom. So let's remember the entire scripture as we seek the kingdom of God. Start listing things that you want for God to add to your territory and leave it to Him. After you have listed those things, go right back to His purpose, seeking His kingdom, and watch those things be added indeed.

It's Your Turn!

What is stopping you from sharing with God the things you'd like for Him to add to your territory? As you think of these things, what would you like to add to your territory for legacy purposes?

"But if God so clothes the grass of the field, which is alive and green today and tomorrow is [cut and] thrown [as fuel] into the furnace, will He not much more clothe you? You of little faith! Therefore do not worry or be anxious (perpetually uneasy, distracted), saying, 'What are we going to eat?' or 'What are we going to drink?' or 'What are we going to wear?' But first and most importantly seek (aim at, strive after)

His kingdom and His righteousness [His way of doing and being right--the attitude and character of God], and all these things will be given to you also."
(Matthew 6:30–33, AMP)

Name Your Excuse

Take thirty seconds to list all the excuses for why you can't save funds for emergencies, invest for your retirement, obtain adequate life insurance to protect your family, or start your own business on one side. In three, two, one, go!

Now on the other side, write down why each excuse is bigger than the God you serve. Take as much time as you need here. *Spoiler alert!* There is nothing, and I mean nothing, greater than our Lord and Savior Jesus Christ!

Now that we've gotten that out of the way, let's not focus on the problems but on the solutions. Let's consider the desire He gave you to be financially secure and maybe even start your own business. Begin saving something starting today. Even if it takes you six months to acquire some savings; God honors your steps, but you have to take a step! Put money to the side in those areas listed above, even if you sacrifice something you like. Maybe that sacrifice is eating out, shopping, and even impulse buying. If you're like me, this would have been something that kept us from reaching our financial goals if we did not make the sacrifices early. I promise God will help you get disciplined. Notice I said the word *help*. I didn't say that He would do it for you. Get your finances in order in such a way that if all goes wrong for a month or two, you have enough in reserves and multiple streams built, to sustain you until your next opportunity to receive income.

It's Your Turn!

What did you write down as your excuses?
Why did you believe you couldn't overcome them?
How much can you commit to putting aside for your future and maybe even your business today?

> *"Whoever loves discipline loves knowledge,*
> *but he who hates reproof is stupid."*
> *(Proverbs 12:1, ESV)*
> *Please note that I didn't call *you* stupid.

Give

What's Your Source?

A braham was pushed to the edge. God asked him to sacrifice the son he loved, not just someone there was no relationship with. We all know they found a ram in the bush and that the ram was sacrificed instead of Isaac. The Lord provided! Why did He tell Abraham to sacrifice His son? Trust and obedience are hard, and they reveal what's in our hearts. He didn't cry on the way to sacrifice His son nor did he have an attitude. If Abraham can endeavor to sacrifice His son with a clean heart, how much more should we be able to sacrifice a few dollars to our God? We have the wrong mind-set about money. *"We made this money so that we can do A, B, and C with it. We earned it ourselves and we deserve to buy X, Y, and Z."* We have gotten so far away from our source. Remember when you prayed to get that job? Who answered your prayers? Your source! Remember when you got laid off? Who kept you and blessed you with that new job just in time? Your source! How dare we become so arrogant that we do not give God at least a tenth of what He gave us?

It's Your Turn!

What is your tenth or tithe?
What have you elevated over God to prevent you from giving your tithe?
What will you commit to give back to God?

"And Abraham lifted up His eyes, and looked, and, behold, behind him a ram caught in the thicket by His horns: and Abraham went and took the ram, and offered him up for a burnt-offering in the stead of His son. And Abraham called the name of that place Jehovah-jireh: as it is said to this day, in the mount of Jehovah it shall be provided."
(Genesis 22:13–14, ASV)

Why the Attitude?

Do you feel like tithing is an obligation that works a nerve? Do you feel if you don't pay your tithe, you'll get got by God? Some feel He's waiting on us to be just shy of the tenth so He can punish us. You may have family members who still believe in that kind of God. However, I have found in God's Word that "each gives as he purposes in his heart and not grudgingly." We have also heard many times that God loves a cheerful giver. We should want to give to God's work in our local churches, to help others, and give thanks to our Source. It's not just about the amount of money, but the cheerful attitudes we have while giving that blesses God. Let's trust Him completely and give with a cheerful heart.

It's Your Turn!

What is your attitude about giving?
Do you give cheerfully or grudgingly?
What can you do today to change your attitude about giving in the future?

> *"But this I say: He who sows sparingly will also reap sparingly, and he who sows bountifully will also reap bountifully. So let each one give as he purposes in his heart, not grudgingly or of necessity; for God loves a cheerful giver."*
> *(2 Corinthians 9:6–7, NKJV)*

Who Are You Robbing?

We all know the scripture Malachi 3:8–9. Don't roll your eyes here. I recognize some of us were taught that if we don't tithe, God will punish us by making something bad happen, like your car will break down or you'll have to go to the hospital. Then the money you spent in those situations would equal what you should have given to a church. I hate to disappoint you. I tithe, and yet these things happen to me too. So is God getting me for tithing? That sounds silly, right? God is a Father, the Good Father. He is not a sperm donor. He does allow things in our lives to make us wiser and stronger. However, He's not waiting for us to disobey Him so He can get us. If we continue reading this passage, we find He gives us two reasons why we should give:

- "So there may be food in my house." He is letting us know that tithing and offerings are to be used as a provision for those in our community in need. I believe *food* can also refer to His Word. We're robbing God's creation when we don't give tithes and offerings to local churches and charitable organizations.

- "Until there is no more need." Here's the reward for us! God's giving us a chance to be generous so He can bless us too. He's so serious about this, He encourages us to test Him. The reward should never be our motivation, but we should understand it is a by-product of our giving. We are robbing ourselves when we don't give. Let's not miss out on God's reward.

Additionally, we may be robbing ourselves in tax deductions. In many cases, giving to local churches and other charitable organizations may help lower taxable income, thereby lowering what is owed at tax time or possibly increasing tax returns. It's worth speaking with a certified public accountant to learn more about this valuable opportunity.

It's Your Turn!

What keeps you from tithing or giving to your local church or charitable organizations?

What can you commit to today to start giving or possibly giving more to your local church or charitable organizations?

How do you feel now that this issue is settled in your heart?

> *"Will man rob God? Yet you are robbing me. But you say, 'How have we robbed you?' In your tithes and contributions. You are cursed with a curse, for you are robbing me, the whole nation of you. Bring the full tithe into the storehouse, that there may be food in my house. And thereby put me to the test, says the Lord of hosts, if I will not open the windows of heaven for you and pour down for you a blessing until there is no more need."*
> *(Malachi 3:8–10, ESV)*

Notes

I Would If I Could,
but I Can't So

I've heard this phrase all my life. You may even be able to complete this sentence too. I've been at this point in my tithing. I felt that since I didn't have enough for tithing, I would negate it all together. What I failed to realize is that I had it but misman-aged what I had. I allowed instant gratification to overwhelm my finances and didn't even know it. I had a car payment with a high-interest rate, high monthly phone bill, and credit cards I was working to pay off with almost no real results. I was forced to really look at my lifestyle and understand that my life-style was keeping me from God's design of living an abundant life. It's not just about the material increase but increase in all aspects of my life. However, it all started as I decided to live well beneath my means by concentrating on my needs versus my wants. As I did, I began to finally give some and work up to the tenth. God kept me and honored my giving in that season. I found that once I gave cheerfully and trusted Him, He began to start forgiving my debts.

I had been paying one company for over a year and they didn't even see my profile anymore. I had not been sent to the collection agency or anything. The debt was totally forgiven and forgotten! As I discovered this was tied to my heart for giving, I gave more and built up to my 10 percent. God continues to bless time after time. As I got married and my family grew, we continued at 10 percent, then started to give sacrificially. We can bless others only because I began to properly manage the little I had all those years ago and give God back to Him a small portion of what He gave me.

It's Your Turn!

What can you give up to give more?
When was the last time you found that God honors your giving?
What made you stop giving?
How has God blessed you in such a way you were inspired to give more?

"'And I will rebuke the devourer for your sakes, So that he will not destroy the fruit of your ground, Nor shall the vine fail to bear fruit for you in the field,'
Says the Lord of hosts;
'And all nations will call you blessed, For you will be a delightful land,'
Says the Lord of hosts."
(Malachi 3:11–12, NKJV)

IT'S YOUR TURN

Notes

Why Not Me?

Many people believe they aren't supposed to accumulate wealth, that this idea is selfish. In the words of my bishop, Dr. Derek Grier, "This is foreign to scripture." There are many examples in the Bible where God's people became prosperous. However, they were obedient to God. I didn't say they were perfect. God's people didn't hoard their money. In fact, the Bible discusses the cheerful giver. The cheerful giver has made it their obligation to give. Why? To bring glory to God! So ask yourself, "Why not me?" You are *the* King's kid and you're supposed to accumulate wealth. Be a giver so God's glory can reign here on your earth.

It's Your Turn!

When was the last time you searched God's Word concerning your finances?
Do you believe God wants you to experience abundant living? Why or why not?
What is your attitude toward giving?
When was the last time you gave cheerfully?

"And God is able to make all grace abound to you,
so that having all sufficiency in all things at all
times, you may abound in every good work. As it
is written, 'He has distributed freely, he has given
to the poor; His righteousness endures forever."
(2 Corinthians 9:8–9, ESV)

No High Beams

As I drive Virginia back roads home at night, I need to have my high-beam lights on. I don't feel safe without being able to see where I'm going. Otherwise, the ride home will be a very long and slow one for me and for those behind me. Well, it doesn't work that way all the time when it comes to your finances if you're following God. There are no high beams to disclose the road ahead. Many unexpected things will happen! Flat tires, medical expenses, house repairs, and the list goes on. The Bible says that His Word is a light unto our path and a lamp to our feet. No high beams here! The Lord gives us what we need as we take each step. His wisdom ensures we lean on Him and not trust in money. Had He shown me where I'd be today, I wouldn't have even tried to be disciplined with my money. I thank Him because I wouldn't be able to fulfill my purpose today without Him making me do things His way. I trust Him with life and money without the high beams!

It's Your Turn!

What keeps you from trusting God with your money?
What financial areas do you like high beams in?
What control are you willing to relinquish concerning your finances?

> *"Your word is a lamp to my feet and a light
> to my path. I have sworn and confirmed that
> I will keep Your righteous judgments."*
> *(Psalms 119:105–106, NKJV)*

Where's Your Seed?

When was the last time you gave to something or someone because you felt bad or felt like you should? Did you consult God? If you're like I was, I didn't think that I needed to consult with God on my *every* move, especially on where I gave *my* money. There's something of concern with that thought process—*my* money? We already know that it's God who provides, including money. Therefore, it benefits us to ask Him what we should do with it. The Bible speaks about sowing seed on good ground versus bad ground. This parable speaks of the Word of God, but I believe you can apply this same principle to your finances. I know when I put my seed in bad soil, the money I had left was negatively affected by my poor decision. Once, my husband was interested in a get-rich-quick scheme as it turned out. We bought the materials and started calling our program mentors. Long story short, we would have had to pay an additional $3,000 to get the results we saw on the infomercial. My husband was all for it. I'm *always* the skeptical one. God came through the phone lines and kept disconnecting our phone call. After the third disconnection, we knew that God was trying to prevent us from making a critical mistake. On the contrary, when we began to ask God for wisdom on where to give *His* money, we started being blessed beyond belief and still reap the benefits today!

It's Your Turn!

What has God told you about where to plant your seed? What keeps you from being obedient to His Word and guidance?
If you've been obedient, have you shared your testimony? Why or why not?

> *"Other seeds fell among thorns, and the thorns grew up and choked them. Other seeds fell on good soil and produced grain, some a hundredfold, some sixty, some thirty." (Matthew 13:7–8, ESV)*

See It My Way

Sometimes, the world has it right when it comes to money. We see people who may or may not believe in Jesus yet give to charity, build businesses, and come up with fantastic ideas or inventions that earn millions of dollars. Some of us Christians gripe about those who have money and even condemn them but won't do what's necessary to earn that kind of money ourselves. We're King's kids. If those who don't know Jesus can create wealth, why can't we? Additionally, we have our Bibles to show us how much more prosperous we'd be when we're generous to God's kingdom. Wouldn't it be awesome to see an interview of someone who earned much success share how God helped them? I bet that would encourage you! Why can't that be you?

It's Your Turn!

What idea, business, or gift has God told you to walk in, but you haven't?

What's stopping you?

Do you feel as if lack of money is keeping you from realizing your idea, business, or gift?

How did God tell you to operate in your idea, business, or gift?

"For the ministry of this service is not only supplying the needs of the saints but is also overflowing in many thanksgivings to God. By their approval of this service, they will glorify God because of your submission that comes from your confession of the gospel of Christ, and the generosity of your contribution for them and for all others, while they long for you and pray for you, because of the surpassing grace of God upon you. Thanks be to God for His inexpressible gift!"
(2 Corinthians 9:12–15, ESV)

Have Faith

God's Word shows us what faith is. It teaches us that we should focus and believe on God's promises and not what we see with our natural eyes. This should really encourage us to exercise that same faith even in our finances. God declares that we can test Him in this one area and watch as He meets our needs. I remember testing Him in this area. The Lord told my husband and me to give extra money to our church to move to a larger location. We desired to give what the Lord said to give, but our bank account didn't match what He told us to give. We worried at first, but we finally trusted Him with His direction. As we started to trust God's Word, the Lord began releasing funds from our mortgage that we unknowingly overpaid, gave us extreme savings on all our expenses, and making our money do more with less. We couldn't have given like He directed unless we had His help! He made a way for us to give what He told us to give. However, nothing happened until we agreed with His Word and was obedient to God. Our faith is stronger now because we exercised His Word and experienced His promise.

It's Your Turn!

What keeps you from believing God about your finances and giving?

When was the last time you trusted and obeyed God's Word in an area and witnessed His promise came to pass? Why are your finances different?

Who have you shared your faith with in this area that gave them the encouragement to exercise their faith in finances?

"Praise the Lord! Blessed is the man who fears the Lord, who greatly delights in His commandments! His offspring will be mighty in the land; the generation of the upright will be blessed. Wealth and riches are in His house, and His righteousness endures forever."
(Psalms 112:1–3, ESV)

I Don't Have
Enough to Give

The devil is a liar! If you go to work and earn income, you have enough to give. In fact, you've been giving to yourself in the form of instant gratification. *"How? I deserve to have fun. I'm gonna take myself to dinner. I work hard, and I'm getting this designer purse!"* There's nothing wrong with having fun, eating out, and getting nice things every now and then. However; things should not be above giving back to God what He gave us! The Bible discusses loving God by putting money where our treasure is and loving our neighbor as ourselves. Our giving should be toward a Godly purpose that helps others and proves that God is first in our lives. Next, we should be wise about managing the money He provided. He expects us to live good lives and to consider life in retirement, leaving an inheritance for our legacy, and storing up treasures in heaven. We all fall short in this area at times, but let's commit to prioritizing our treasure. Put your treasure in Him first so He can show you that His treasure is in you!

It's Your Turn!

When was the last time you took a look at your transactions and saw where most of your money is going?
How much are you willing to commit to His work on earth, starting with your local church?
How much are you willing to commit to in order to leave a legacy through various means?

"Do not lay up for yourselves treasures on earth, where moth and rust destroy and where thieves break in and steal, but lay up for yourselves treasures in heaven, where neither moth nor rust destroys and where thieves do not break in and steal. For where your treasure is, there your heart will be also."
(Matthew 6:19–21, ESV)

If You Do Nothing, Nothing Will Change

At our church, we have three major opportunities to give extra offerings each year. At first, we didn't give these offering opportunities much thought. However, our family's finances were seriously out of order. We weren't praying over our financial decisions and just did what we wanted to without regard for God's Word. It wasn't until my husband and I decided to obey His Word and get our home in order that we realized a level of financial freedom and favor we hadn't yet experienced. As we gave and continued to give more, we've seen and continued to see more blessings over our lives, including our finances. Our relationships with each other, other family members, and others have improved. Everything seemed like it just got better! The process still continues. So was it just us giving money to our church that fixed everything? No. Our hearts changed about giving and saving for our future. Our hearts became committed to God's Word and guidance through the Holy Spirit and then things changed. If we did nothing, nothing would have changed.

It's Your Turn!

What keeps you from changing your attitude about giving?
Why have you decided to give to your local church?
What evidence has God shown you that He approves of your giving?

> *"Delight yourself in the Lord, and he will give you the desires of your heart. Commit your way to the Lord; trust in him, and he will act."*
> *(Psalms 37:4–5, ESV)*

Give Freely

God has a secret reserved especially for His children: giving is a major key toward financial success. Accordingly to Scripture, God expects us to live life with an open hand. An open hand allows God to give us more because He knows we will give more to His kingdom. We are to represent Him to others through our giving. Money is a small matter to our big God. If He can trust us with little, then He will be able to trust us with much and allow us to use our gifts effectively. If you're not a giver, please don't expect God to give you great results. When you live life to bless others, the Lord will make sure you are blessed. Don't be afraid to give freely. Your journey to financial success starts by letting go.

It's Your Turn!

How have you practiced giving freely?
What keeps you from trusting that giving freely is where your financial success begins?
How can you commit to a new attitude of giving freely?

> *"One gives freely, yet grows all the richer; another withholds what he should give, and only suffers want. Whoever brings blessing will be enriched, and one who waters will himself be watered."*
> *(Proverbs 11:24–25, ESV)*

Why Keep It to Yourself? (The Remix)

When was the last time you saw a good movie or ate at an excellent restaurant? Have you ever visited a place you couldn't wait to get back home to tell all your friends and family about? I know when I experience something extravagant or amazing, I enjoy sharing my thoughts and excitement about that experience. As Jesus healed people, they couldn't help but tell everyone about it! More than likely you do the same thing. So why aren't we like this when it comes to receiving good information about our finances? Jesus told us His strategies on how to be successful with our finances. Why do we keep these good things to ourselves?

It may be because you:

      A: hadn't sought the information

      B: tried something good half-heartedly and claimed it failed and/or

      C: want to outdo or one up your friends and peers

I like to say, "Friends shouldn't let friends retire broke." If you want to be financially successful, first look to God's Word, then find yourself a licensed expert and someone you can trust to be the example for you to follow. I am not threatened if someone has more in their financial portfolio than I do or if they are striving to increase the current portfolio. There is enough room for all of us. Let us lift each other up and work to enjoy life like no one else!

It's Your Turn!

What good financial tips have you received that were successful and you shared with someone else?
When was the last time you encouraged friends or coworkers to take care of themselves financially?

"And he did not permit him but said to him, 'Go home to your friends and tell them how much the Lord has done for you, and how he has had mercy on you.' And he went away and began to proclaim in the Decapolis how much Jesus had done for him, and everyone marveled."
(Mark 5:19–20, ESV)

Don't Look Back

I know how difficult changing habits can be. You have become accustomed to consistently doing things one way for a long time. Even though we may have discovered a new and maybe even better way, we can still be hesitant or fearful of leaving the old and comfortable. Changing financial habits can be just as frightening. However, what are the negative consequences of saving money for emergencies? What about saving for retirement? How about making sure your family is not in financial chaos because you passed away unexpectedly? What about giving more to God's Kingdom? Any negative consequences there? These are all positive moves toward establishing your financial foundation. Make a decision to abandon old spending habits and adopt new ones to secure yourself and your family financially. Once you've taken that step, don't look back. The best is ahead of you!

It's Your Turn!

What keeps you paralyzed from stepping away from bad spending habits?

What habits can you adopt to help your current financial situation?

What can you commit to today to change your bad spending habits?

> *"But Lot's wife, behind him, looked back,*
> *and she became a pillar of salt."*
> *(Genesis 19:26, ESV)*

The Last Domino

I 've talked to a lot of people who have been a financial pillar in their family for too many years. By the time I sit down and speak with them, they are just plain sick and tired of being sick and tired of lending money to family members or close friends because it's gotten them nowhere financially. Also, by this time, they are in a mountain of debt because they continued to give money away expecting repayment that never came. They're frustrated because they see these friends or family members going on vacations, buying new cars, or new wardrobes while still owing money to the person that lent them the money in the first place. So I asked this one simple question, "Who do you have to lean on if you are in a financial crisis?" They pause for a moment or two. After a pause, I already know what the answer is. I call that person the Last Domino. Is this person you? If so, what type of financial strain has this cost you? Think about it. Then also think about the negative consequences this has caused. What financial gain have you seen by lending people money and never getting repaid? I know this is a very hard pill to swallow. Very hard. Still, consider where this string of decisions has landed you financially. Now that you have, let's resolve to make sure the Last Domino stands strong on its own.

It's Your Turn!

When was the last time allowed someone to borrow money from you?

If you got the money back, how long did it take? If you did not get that money back, what financial position did that put you in?

What could have been a better way to use that money so that when a financial crisis hit your home you had enough in emergency savings to withstand the situation?

"The wicked borrows and does not repay, but the righteous shows mercy and gives. For those blessed by Him shall inherit the earth, But those cursed by Him shall be cut off." (Psalms 37:21–22, NKJV)
*Please note I did not call your friends and family members wicked.

Notes

The End

You have withstood our time together. I pray that this book has given you some biblical and practical insight on how to start or return to your financial journey. You answered some tough questions and possibly made even tougher decisions to positively impact your financial journey. Now take this information and gather the courage that you gained during our time together to go for it! Take three minutes and close your eyes. Think about the end of your financial road. Now that you've taken some small, simple steps, you're on that road! Where do you see yourself at that end? Don't give up, don't turn back, and keep moving forward! I can't wait to high-five you at the end of your race! Now, seriously . . .

It is indeed your turn!

With all my love, Tina

About the Author

Tina Smith is a licensed financial planner. She is an investment advisor representative and a health and life insurance agent for multiple states across the country. Having been a long-time client of her financial planning firm, she understands the importance of having a financial planner and a comprehensive family financial plan. She serves as a deacon in her church, where she teaches biblical and practical financial principles. She shares these same principles with multiple churches in the Commonwealth of Virginia. Tina is also a retiree of the United States Air Force. She is married to Karshi, and they have one son, Anthony.